WORLD'S STRANGEST

CREEPY-CRAWLIES

Produced for Lonely Planet by Plum5 Limited
Authors: Stuart Derrick & Charlotte Goddard
Editor: Plum5 Limited
Designer: Plum5 Limited
Publishing Director: Piers Pickard
Art Director: Andy Mansfield
Commissioning Editors: Catharine Robertson, Jen Feroze
Assistant Editor: Christina Webb
Print Production: Nigel Longuet, Lisa Ford
With thanks to: Jennifer Dixon

Published in August 2018 by Lonely Planet Global Ltd

CRN: 554153
ISBN: 978 1 78701 298 1

www.lonelyplanetkids.com
© Lonely Planet 2018

Printed in China
2 4 6 8 10 9 7 5 3 1

STAY IN TOUCH – lonelyplanet.com/contact
Lonely Planet Offices
AUSTRALIA the Malt Store, Level 3, 551 Swanston St, Carlton, Victoria 3053   t: 03 8379 8000
IRELAND Digital Depot, Roe Lane (off Thomas St), Digital Hub, Dublin 8, D08 TCV4
USA 124 Linden St, Oakland, CA 94607 t: 510 250 6400
UK 240 Blackfriars Rd, London SE1 8NW t: 020 3771 5100

WORLD'S STRANGEST
CREEPY-CRAWLIES

Stuart Derrick &
Charlotte Goddard

PICTURE CREDITS

The Publisher would like to thank the following for their kind permission to reproduce their photographs:

Page 4–5: Shutterstock / Sugarless; Page 6–7: Shutterstock / Zoran Milosavljevic; Page 8–9: Andy Myatt / Alamy Stock Photo; Page 8 inset: Getty images / Gary Braasch / Corbis; Page 10–11: Shutterstock / PJ_joe; Page 12: Shutterstock / Martin Pelanek; Page 13: Shutterstock / GR Photo; Page 14–15: The Natural History Museum / Alamy Stock Photo; Page 16: Getty images / picture by la-ong; Page 16 inset: Shutterstock / Waravut Watanapanich; Page 17: Shutterstock / G Talley; Page 17 inset: Shutterstock / Betty Shelton; Page 18–19: blickwinkel / Alamy Stock Photo; Page 20: Rob Cleary / OEH; Page 21: Photo Resource Hawaii / Alamy Stock Photo; Page 22–23: Shutterstock / funnyangel; Page 22 inset: Rob Cleary / OEH; Page 23 inset: Shutterstock / PJ_joe; Page 24–25: 500px / 惟迪 张; Page 26–27: Shutterstock / Martin Pelanek; Page 28–29: 500px / Sreekumar Mahadevan Pillai; Page 29 inset: Getty images / Adegsm; Page 30: 500px / Manoj Kumar Tuteja; Page 31: Getty images / Billy Currie Photography; Page 32–33: Getty images / Sandra Standbridge; Page 33 inset: Wayne HUTCHINSON / Alamy Stock Photo; Page 34: Vasiliy Vishnevskiy / Alamy Stock Photo; Page 35: Getty images / Michael Marsh / stocks photography/; Page 36–37: Shutterstock / fntproject; Page 37 inset: Shutterstock / Dmitri Gomon; Page 38–39: Shutterstock / Bildagentur Zoonar GmbH; Page 22–23: Shutterstock / funnyangel; Page 40 inset: Shutterstock / fntproject; Page 41 inset: 500px / Sreekumar Mahadevan Pillai; Page 42–43: Shutterstock / cyrrpit; Page 44–45: louise murray / Alamy Stock Photo; Page 46: Getty images / Larry Sinanto / EyeEm; Page 46 inset: Getty images / Javier Fernández Sánchez; Page 47: Shutterstock / Ruzy Hartini; Page 48–49: Shutterstock / Vladimir Wrangel; Page 49 inset: Shutterstock / Shinelu2; Page 50–51: Shutterstock / IrinaK; Page 50 inset: Shutterstock / Brett Hondow; Page 52: Getty / EcoPic; Page 53: Shutterstock / neil hardwick; Page 54–55: Getty images / George Grall; Page 55 inset: Shutterstock / Christian Vinces; Page 56–57: Getty images / tomosang; Page 56 inset: Shutterstock / WUT. ANUNAI; Page 22–23: Shutterstock / funnyangel; Page 58 inset: Getty / EcoPic; Page 59 inset: Getty images / Larry Sinanto / EyeEm; Page 60–61: Getty images / George Grall; Page 61 inset: Shutterstock / Jason Patrick Ross; Page 62–63: Survivalphotos / Alamy Stock Photo; Page 63 inset: Shutterstock / tuasiwatn; Page 64–65: Getty images / somnuk krobkum; Page 66: Getty images / Flick's Pix; Page 67: Shutterstock / exOrzist; Page 68–69: Shutterstock / Matt Jeppson; Page 68 inset: Shutterstock / Piyavachara Nacchanandana; Page 70–71: Getty images / Aukid Phumsirichat / EyeEm; Page 70 inset: Shutterstock / Herman Wong HM; Page 72–73: Patrick Landmann / Science Photo Library; Page 73 inset: Patrick Landmann / Science Photo Library; Page 74–75: WILDLIFE GmbH / Alamy Stock Photo; Page 74 inset: Shutterstock / Peter Reijners; Page 76–77: D. Magdalena Sorger / www.theantlife.com; Page 78–79: Shutterstock / funnyangel; Page 78 inset: Getty images / George Grall; Page 79 inset: Shutterstock / exOrzist; Page 80: Shutterstock / Nik Merkulov.

CONTENTS

INTRODUCTION 6

CREEPY-CRAWLIES #40-31

ELEPHANT BEETLE..................... 8
MILLIPEDE 10
CADDISFLY......................... 12
QUEEN ALEXANDRA'S BIRDWING....... 13
FAIRYFLY 14

JEWEL BEETLE 16
HICKORY HORNED DEVIL 17
GIANT GIPPSLAND EARTHWORM 18
HOT-PINK SLUG..................... 20
HAPPY-FACE SPIDER................. 21

QUIZ 22

CREEPY-CRAWLIES #30-21

ZOMBIE SNAIL 24
LESSER WATER BOATMAN 26
WEAVER ANT 28
MIRROR SPIDER 30
LEAFCUTTER ANT 31

FROGHOPPER 32
GLOBE SKIMMER 34
HONEY BEE 35
GOLIATH BEETLE 36
SPINY DEVIL KATYDID 38

QUIZ 40

CREEPY-CRAWLIES #20-11

GOLIATH BIRDEATER 42
GIANT WETA 44
MOUND-BUILDING TERMITE............ 46
ASIAN GIANT HORNET 47
LOCUST 48

ASP CATERPILLAR 50
SCORPION 52
PUSS MOTH CATERPILLAR 53
THORN BUG......................... 54
FIREFLY 56

QUIZ 58

CREEPY-CRAWLIES #10-1

EASTERN DOBSONFLY................. 60
DEATH'S-HEAD HAWK MOTH 62
LEAF INSECT 64
GLASSWING BUTTERFLY 66
BIRD-DUNG CRAB SPIDER 67

GIANT SILKWORM MOTH CATERPILLAR .. 68
ASSASSIN BUG 70
BRAZILIAN TREEHOPPER.............. 72
DEVIL'S FLOWER MANTIS............. 74
EXPLODING ANT 76

QUIZ 78

GLOSSARY 80

INTRODUCTION

They might be hard to see sometimes, but insects make up 80 percent of all the world's species. It is estimated that there are 10 quintillion insects alive – that's 10,000,000,000,000,000,000, or 10 billion billion, creepy-crawlies.

Of course, not all creepy-crawlies are insects. There are 47,500 spider species alone, as well as earthworms, millipedes, and many other different kinds of creatures. This book ranks some of the strangest, by looking at...

⭐ The amazing ways they hide from view

⭐ The astonishing powers of these mighty mini-beasts

⭐ How ferocious they are

Read on to find out about some of the strangest creepy-crawlies that you would be lucky, or unlucky, enough to encounter, including:

⭐ The tiny terror that blows itself up to save its friends

⭐ A crazy snail that turns into a zombie

⭐ A creature that is so well disguised even its own species can't spot it

⭐ A monstrous spider that's as big as a dinner plate

... and lots more of the world's most fantastically strange creepy-crawlies.

STRANGEOMETER

The creatures in this book are all unique in their own ways, so we've used a special strangeometer to rank them. This is made up of four categories with a score out of 25 for each.

These categories are...

STRANGEOMETER

 CREEPINESS — 17/25

 SUPERPOWERS — 8/25

 BUG BEAUTY — 12/25

 FIGHT FACTOR — 13/25

 STRANGEOMETER SCORE — 50/100

CREEPINESS

How likely are they to make you shiver?

SUPERPOWERS

What special skills do these creatures have to make them stand out from the norm?

BUG BEAUTY

You might think some bugs are ugly, but how good-looking are these lovely creatures?

FIGHT FACTOR

They might be small, but how much fight do they have?

STRANGEOMETER SCORE

These are added up to get a strangeometer score out of 100!

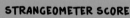

#40

Male elephant beetles have horns like elephant tusks, which they use to fight for female mates and food.

I LIKE MY FOOD TO BE ROTTEN AND DECAYING.

Mexico, and Central and South American rainforests

Scientists are turning elephant beetles into cyborg robots. The beetles are strong enough to carry a backpack that allows them to be controlled with a video game handset. It's all in a good cause – hopefully, the flying insects will be able to take part in rescue missions and find people trapped in rubble after earthquakes or explosions. They might even be able to help track down criminals!

ELEPHANT
BEETLE

The elephant beetle is one of the giants of the insect world, ranging from 3–5 in. (8–13 cm) long! Don't worry, they may look fierce but they only eat fruit and flowers.

STRANGEOMETER

CREEPINESS		5/25
SUPERPOWERS		9/25
BUG BEAUTY		14/25
FIGHT FACTOR		3/25
STRANGEOMETER SCORE		31/100

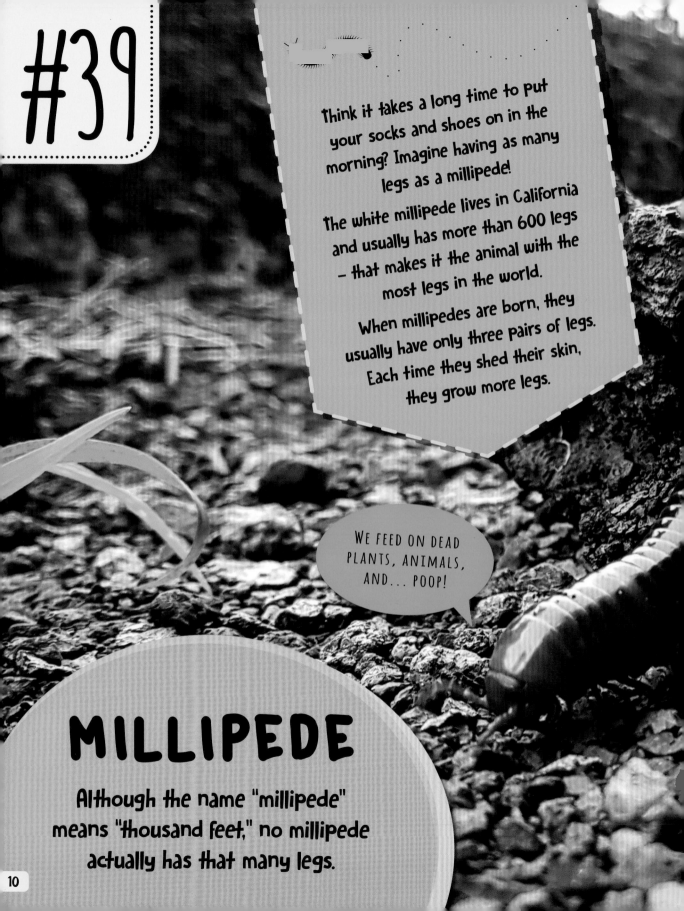

Think it takes a long time to put your socks and shoes on in the morning? Imagine having as many legs as a millipede!

The white millipede lives in California and usually has more than 600 legs – that makes it the animal with the most legs in the world.

When millipedes are born, they usually have only three pairs of legs. Each time they shed their skin, they grow more legs.

WE FEED ON DEAD PLANTS, ANIMALS, AND... POOP!

MILLIPEDE

Although the name "millipede" means "thousand feet," no millipede actually has that many legs.

Every continent except Antarctica

STRANGEOMETER

CREEPINESS		10/25
SUPERPOWERS		2/25
BUG BEAUTY		18/25
FIGHT FACTOR		2/25
STRANGEOMETER SCORE		32/100

#38 CADDISFLY

There are thousands of different caddisfly species. Their young (larvae) live in rivers, lakes, and ponds.

Freshwater habitats on every continent except Antarctica

STRANGEOMETER

CREEPINESS	3/25
SUPERPOWERS	18/25
BUG BEAUTY	10/25
FIGHT FACTOR	2/25
STRANGEOMETER SCORE	33/100

WHEN WE ARE READY TO GROW UP, WE CLOSE OUR SUIT OF ARMOR LIKE A COCOON AND BITE OUR WAY OUT.

Baby caddisflies are soft and squidgy. This is dangerous when their ponds are full of fish that want to eat them! The crafty little larvae make their own suits of armor out of silk and whatever they can find lying around – such as twigs, sand, and gravel.

Would you wear a necklace made by a creepy-crawly? Some caddisflies make their suits out of gems instead of twigs, and jewelry-makers turn them into pretty decorations.

QUEEN ALEXANDRA'S BIRDWING

Imagine butterflies as large as dinner plates flitting around, and you have an idea of how huge the Queen Alexandra's birdwing is! These monster butterflies are the biggest in the world.

I'M VERY RARE! WHEN A VOLCANO ERUPTED NEARLY 70 YEARS AGO, IT DESTROYED A BIG PART OF MY HOME.

Papua New Guinea

You won't see these giant butterflies fluttering around your garden – unless you live in a small area of rainforest in Papua New Guinea. This is the only place on the planet where the Queen Alexandra's birdwing can be found.

STRANGEOMETER

CREEPINESS		6/25
SUPERPOWERS		5/25
BUG BEAUTY		22/25
FIGHT FACTOR		3/25
STRANGEOMETER SCORE		36/100

#36

We were around at the same time as the dinosaurs!

Fairyflies aren't fairies or flies, but a type of wasp. They live inside the eggs of other insects and eventually kill their hosts.

Fairyflies don't have a magic wand, but some of them do have beautiful wings. There are about 1,424 different kinds of fairyfly. One of them is called *Tinkerbella nana*, after the fairy in *Peter Pan*. It is found in Costa Rica.

Temperate climates across the world

FAIRYFLY

Fairyflies are the tiniest insects in the world, measuring only 0.02 in. (0.5 mm).

Fairyflies are all around us, but they are so small that people don't usually notice them. Some of them are only as big as the tip of a pen. They only live for a few days, so that makes them even harder to track down.

STRANGEOMETER

 CREEPINESS — 12/25

 SUPERPOWERS — 8/25

 BUG BEAUTY — 10/25

 FIGHT FACTOR — 7/25

STRANGEOMETER SCORE — 37/100

HELLO, I'M HERE! HAVE A LOOK ON THIS RULER TO SEE JUST HOW SMALL WE ARE!

JEWEL BEETLE

There are around 15,000 different kinds of jewel beetle. Many have bright, shimmering colors, such as metallic greens and reds.

STRANGEOMETER

CREEPINESS		1/25
SUPERPOWERS		8/25
BUG BEAUTY		25/25
FIGHT FACTOR		8/25
STRANGEOMETER SCORE		42/100

Most animals run away from fires, but jewel beetles fly straight towards them. They need freshly burned wood to lay their eggs and so have developed amazing sensors that can detect flames from as far as 50 miles (80 km) away.

Every continent except Antarctica

WE'RE SO PRETTY, THE VICTORIANS USED TO WEAR US AS BROOCHES.

Despite its weird appearance and scary name, the hickory horned devil is harmless. Its spikes are prickly but they don't sting. It's a pretty big bug though – the size of a hot dog!

> I EAT LOTS OF HICKORY LEAVES. ONCE I'M A MOTH, I CAN'T EAT ANY MORE, BECAUSE I WON'T HAVE A MOUTH.

HICKORY HORNED DEVIL

The hickory horned devil is the caterpillar of the regal moth, also known as the royal walnut moth.

Eastern US

STRANGEOMETER

CREEPINESS		13/25
SUPERPOWERS		5/25
BUG BEAUTY		25/25
FIGHT FACTOR		0/25
STRANGEOMETER SCORE		43/100

17

#33

If you hear a noise under your feet like water draining out of a bath, that might be a giant Gippsland earthworm. They make a strange sucking noise as they wriggle through their underground burrows!

Australia

GIANT GIPPSLAND
EARTHWORM

When workers building a railroad first found the giant Gippsland earthworm around 150 years ago, they thought it was a snake, but it's actually a 3.3 ft. long (1 m long) worm.

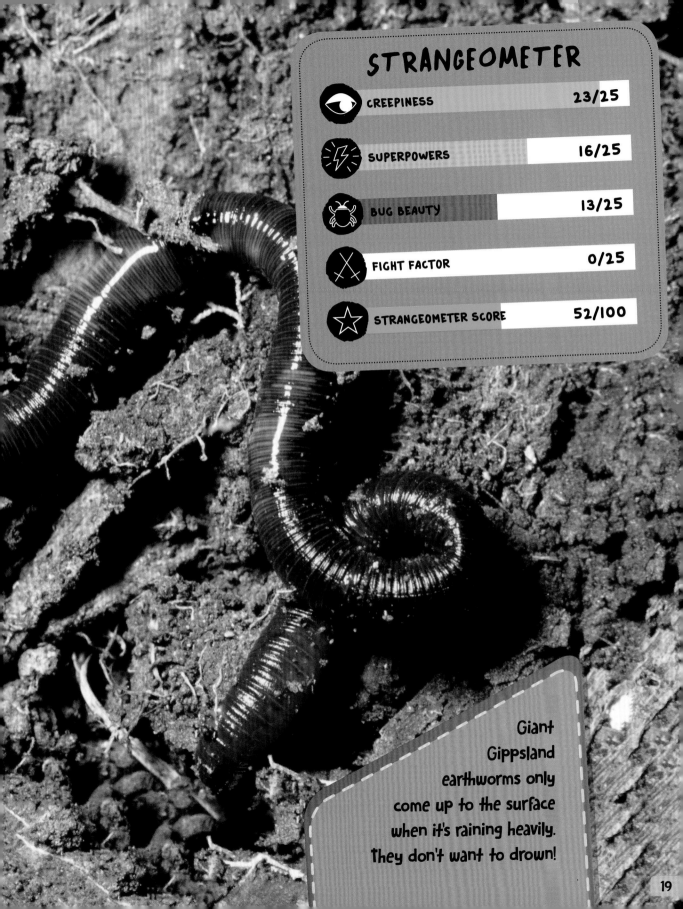

STRANGEOMETER

CREEPINESS		23/25
SUPERPOWERS		16/25
BUG BEAUTY		13/25
FIGHT FACTOR		0/25
STRANGEOMETER SCORE		52/100

Giant Gippsland earthworms only come up to the surface when it's raining heavily. They don't want to drown!

#32

It's slimy, it's yucky, and it's bright pink! Scientists think that the pink color could be camouflage, as the slugs live in beds of red eucalyptus leaves.

WE EAT MOSS AND MOLD THAT GROW ON TREE TRUNKS. YUM!

Australia

HOT-PINK SLUG

This 8 in. long (20 cm long) slug is only found on one Australian mountain, Mount Kaputar. Other creepy-crawlies that only live on that mountain include the Kaputar hairy snail and the Kaputar cannibal snail.

STRANGEOMETER

CREEPINESS		24/25
SUPERPOWERS		3/25
BUG BEAUTY		25/25
FIGHT FACTOR		3/25
STRANGEOMETER SCORE		55/100

HAPPY-FACE SPIDER

the colors and shapes of the markings on its back are different for every happy-face spider, but many look like smiley faces!

This cheery-looking spider is only 0.2 in. (5 mm) long, so you would need a magnifying glass to see its markings. It lives beneath the leaves of plants.

WE ONLY LIVE HIGH IN THE RAINFORESTS OF HAWAII.

Hawaii

STRANGEOMETER

CREEPINESS		11/25
SUPERPOWERS		12/25
BUG BEAUTY		25/25
FIGHT FACTOR		8/25
STRANGEOMETER SCORE		56/100

21

QUIZ

3.

What did the people who discovered the giant Gippsland earthworm think it was?

What does the hickory horned devil turn into?

1.

4.

Where does the happy-face spider live?

What creepy-crawly is this?

2.

6.
What did the Victorians do with jewel beetles?

7.
What is the world's biggest butterfly?

8.
What do caddisfly larvae use to make a suit of armor?

5.
What type of insect is a fairyfly?

9.
What creepy-crawly is this?

10.
What do elephant beetles eat?

ANSWERS

1. IN THE RAINFORESTS OF HAWAII 2. HOT-PINK SLUG
3. THE REGAL MOTH 4. A SNAKE 5. A WASP 6. THEY WORE THEM
AS BROOCHES 7. QUEEN ALEXANDRA'S BIRDWING 8. THEY STICK
TWIGS, SAND, GRAVEL, OR EVEN GEMS TO THEIR BODIES WITH SILK
9. MILLIPEDE 10. FRUIT AND FLOWERS

23

#30

ZOMBIE SNAIL

Amber snails eat bird poop. That's weird enough you might think, but there's worse to come. Tiny creatures called parasites live in the poop and so they get eaten, too. The parasites then take control of the snail's brain, making them do some very strange things!

The parasites turn the snail's eyestalks into crazy tentacles. Then they make the snail move into the sunlight, where its weird eyes flash a signal to passing birds, saying, "Come and eat me!"

North America and Europe

The parasite living inside the amber snail wants the snail to be eaten so it can get inside bird poop again, and brainwash another snail.

Once a parasite is inside, it takes over the snail's brain, turning it into a zombie. The poor snail has to do whatever the parasite wants!

BIRDS THINK MY COLORFUL EYESTALKS LOOK LIKE YUMMY CATERPILLARS!

STRANGEOMETER

 CREEPINESS
25/25

 SUPERPOWERS
25/25

 BUG BEAUTY
7/25

 FIGHT FACTOR
0/25

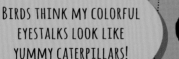 STRANGEOMETER SCORE
57/100

#29

I'M SO LOUD THAT PEOPLE WALKING ON THE RIVERBANK CAN HEAR ME SINGING ON THE RIVERBED.

Central Europe

STRANGEOMETER

 CREEPINESS — 15/25

 SUPERPOWERS — 23/25

 BUG BEAUTY — 10/25

 FIGHT FACTOR — 10/25

 STRANGEOMETER SCORE — 58/100

LESSER WATER BOATMAN

This tiny insect, measuring only 0.01 in. (2 mm), is the loudest animal on Earth for its size.

The lesser water boatman's song is as loud as a passing freight train (78.9 decibels), although scientists have recorded one water boatman bellowing out its song at 99.2 decibels. That's like sitting in the front row at a concert and hearing the orchestra playing! Passers-by are not deafened because the insects sit at the bottom of rivers, and the sound is muffled by the water.

The water boatman carries a bubble of air around to help it breathe underwater!

STRANGEOMETER

 CREEPINESS — 13/25

 SUPERPOWERS — 23/25

 BUG BEAUTY — 11/25

 FIGHT FACTOR — 12/25

 STRANGEOMETER SCORE — 59/100

Africa, India, Southeast Asia, and Australia

Weaver ants are incredibly strong! They have been seen carrying objects that weigh 100 times more than they do – while standing upside-down on a glass surface by holding on with their sticky feet.

OUR COLONIES CAN SPREAD ACROSS MORE THAN 100 NESTS.

WEAVER ANT

Weaver ants use their larvae as glue bottles! They make their nests out of leaves, which they stick together using drops of silk that they gently squeeze out of their little ones.

MIRROR SPIDER

This glam spider's reflective scales look like pieces of mirror stuck onto its back.

Scientists don't know much about mirror spiders, but some think their silvery patches might help the spider hide among the drops of water on a plant.

STRANGEOMETER

CREEPINESS	14/25
SUPERPOWERS	13/25
BUG BEAUTY	25/25
FIGHT FACTOR	8/25
STRANGEOMETER SCORE	60/100

China, Singapore and Southeast Asia, and Australia

I'M ALSO KNOWN AS A SEQUIN SPIDER OR A SILVER DEWDROP SPIDER.

This isn't a disco ball or a piece of jewelry – it's a real spider! The mirror spider's scales can change size when the spider feels threatened.

Leafcutter ants are farmers. They grow their own food in underground fungus farms. The ants travel to find leaves, which they carry home to create fungus. They find their way by sensing the magnetic fields of the Earth, just like a compass!

STRANGEOMETER

👁 CREEPINESS		10/25
⚡ SUPERPOWERS		23/25
🕷 BUG BEAUTY		10/25
✖ FIGHT FACTOR		18/25
★ STRANGEOMETER SCORE		61/100

Southern US, Mexico, Caribbean, and Central and South America

WE USE OUR BIG JAWS TO CUT LEAVES INTO LITTLE BITS.

LEAFCUTTER ANT

Leafcutter ants can carry up to 50 times their body weight. That's like a human carrying a big car!

#25

We suck the sap out of plants!

STRANGEOMETER

 CREEPINESS — 14/25

 SUPERPOWERS — 25/25

 BUG BEAUTY — 16/25

 FIGHT FACTOR — 7/25

 STRANGEOMETER SCORE — 62/100

Froghoppers are very small, less than 0.6 in. (1.5 cm) long.

FROGHOPPER

The froghopper is one of the best jumpers in the insect world. Some can leap up to 27.5 in. (70 cm) in the air.

Europe

When froghoppers jump, they generate a g-force of more than 400 times their own body weight. Astronauts rocketing into orbit only endure a g-force of 6 or 7!

Baby froghoppers cover themselves in frothy bubbles as protection against heat, cold, and predators. People call this froth cuckoo spit or frog spit. Yuck!

#24

GLOBE SKIMMER

The globe skimmer is the highest-flying dragonfly in the world and has been recorded at heights of 20,000 ft. (6,200 m) in the Himalayas.

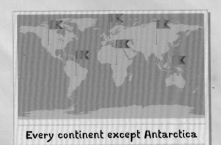

Every continent except Antarctica

I FOLLOW THE WEATHER TO WHERE IT'S NICE AND WET.

STRANGEOMETER

CREEPINESS		10/25
SUPERPOWERS		25/25
BUG BEAUTY		20/25
FIGHT FACTOR		8/25
STRANGEOMETER SCORE		63/100

Globe skimmers are the long-distance travelers of the insect world. They make an epic journey of around 11,000 mi. (18,000 km) every year, crossing oceans from one continent to another!

They may have tiny brains, but honey bees are very clever. Experts are training some bees to find land mines hidden in the ground in places where there have been wars, so that the mines can be removed and the area made safe again.

Every continent except Antarctica

WE CAN RECOGNIZE HUMAN FACES!

HONEY BEE

Honey bees talk to each other by dancing. They do a "waggle dance" to tell other bees where the best flowers are.

STRANGEOMETER

CREEPINESS		8/25
SUPERPOWERS		25/25
BUG BEAUTY		12/25
FIGHT FACTOR		19/25
STRANGEOMETER SCORE		64/100

#22

GOLIATH BEETLE

Africa's Goliath beetle is the heaviest insect in the world. It can weigh up to 3.5 oz. (100 g).

Hunters used to shoot Goliath beetles with rifles. One museum in Africa has several beetles on display with holes in their wings!

Equatorial Africa

WE ARE HEAVIER AS BABIES THAN AS FULLY GROWN ADULTS!

STRANGEOMETER

 CREEPINESS 23/25

 SUPERPOWERS 13/25

 BUG BEAUTY 22/25

 FIGHT FACTOR 8/25

STRANGEOMETER SCORE 66/100

These sluggish giants don't like getting up in the morning – when it's cool, they can't move around much. But once the sun warms them up, they become more active.

STRANGEOMETER

 CREEPINESS — 20/25

 SUPERPOWERS — 15/25

 BUG BEAUTY — 12/25

 FIGHT FACTOR — 20/25

 STRANGEOMETER SCORE — 67/100

The katydid needs protection because it sings so loudly. Experts think it uses its weird spikes to disguise itself as a thorny plant. The spikes also make it difficult to eat – they are sharp enough to draw blood.

SPINY DEVIL
KATYDID

Rainforests of Central and South America

This spiky creature uses its front legs to fight off predators, and has even been seen taking on a small monkey.

THERE ARE MORE THAN 6,400 KINDS OF KATYDID.

During the night, male spiny devils sing a loud, high-pitched song to attract mates. The females put out their front legs to listen – because that's where their ears are!

QUIZ

See if you can answer these questions on the ten creepy-crawlies you've just learned about!

3. Why do honey bees dance?

What do baby froghoppers cover themselves in?

4.

1. Why do spiny devil katydids sing?

2. What creepy-crawly is this?

6. Where do leafcutter ants get their food?

7. What creepy-crawlies are these?

5. How far can globe skimmers fly?

8. What insect has reflective scales?

9. What is the loudest insect for its size?

10. How do parasites control zombie snails?

#20

These furry giants have a strange weapon. They rub their hairy tummies with their legs and flick tiny sharp hairs into the eyes, noses, and mouths of their attackers.

GOLIATH BIRDEATER

The birdeater is the largest spider in the world. With a leg span of up to 11 in. (28 cm), it is about the size of a dinner plate. It can weigh as much as a puppy!

The Goliath birdeater is a kind of tarantula and lives in the rainforests of South America. It has a poisonous bite. Despite its name, this spider rarely eats birds – it's more likely to dig into a tasty worm or snake.

OUR FANGS CAN PIERCE A MOUSE'S SKULL.

Goliath birdeaters don't just look scary – they sound scary, too! These spiders make a loud hissing noise by rubbing the bristles on their legs together.

South America

STRANGEOMETER

CREEPINESS		25/25
SUPERPOWERS		10/25
BUG BEAUTY		8/25
FIGHT FACTOR		25/25
STRANGEOMETER SCORE		68/100

#19 GIANT WETA

One of the biggest insects in the world, the giant weta can weigh the same as three mice!

Giant insects used to be common in New Zealand because there weren't any mammals around to hunt them or take their food.

STRANGEOMETER

 CREEPINESS — 25/25

 SUPERPOWERS — 17/25

 BUG BEAUTY — 15/25

 FIGHT FACTOR — 12/25

 STRANGEOMETER SCORE — 69/100

When rats first arrived in New Zealand on visiting ships, they started to hunt the giant weta. Now there aren't many of these peculiar critters left.

If you want to make friends with a weta, give it a carrot. The massive insects love to munch on them as a snack, using their strong jaws to crunch them.

#18

A group of tiny termites can move a quarter of a ton (250 kg) of soil and several tons of water in a year.

STRANGEOMETER

CREEPINESS	10/25	
SUPERPOWERS	25/25	
BUG BEAUTY	12/25	
FIGHT FACTOR	23/25	
STRANGEOMETER SCORE	70/100	

MOST OF US HAVE NO EYES.

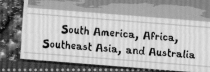

South America, Africa, Southeast Asia, and Australia

A termite queen can produce 1 egg every 3 seconds for 15 years – that's a lot of babies!

MOUND-BUILDING
TERMITE

Termites create amazing structures that look like skyscrapers. Mounds can be 27–30 ft. (8–9 m) high – taller than a two-story house – and can take four or five years to build.

ASIAN GIANT HORNET

Swarms of giant hornets have been known to kill and eat an entire colony of honey bees.

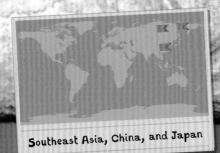

WE'RE KNOWN AS YAK-KILLER HORNETS BECAUSE OF OUR POWERFUL STINGS!

#17

The Asian giant hornet is the largest wasp in the world. It can grow to 2 in. (5.5 cm) long, with a wingspan of around 3 in. (7.6 cm).

Southeast Asia, China, and Japan

The sting of the Asian giant hornet is so powerful it can dissolve human body tissue. Without proper treatment, a single sting can kill a person.

STRANGEOMETER

👁 CREEPINESS		15/25
⚡ SUPERPOWERS		16/25
🪲 BUG BEAUTY		15/25
✖ FIGHT FACTOR		25/25
★ STRANGEOMETER SCORE		71/100

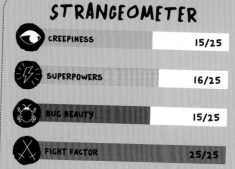

#16

Locust swarms can cover vast distances – in 1988, one swarm traveled from West Africa all the way to the Caribbean.

THE ANCIENT EGYPTIANS PAINTED PICTURES OF US IN THEIR TOMBS TO TRY TO WARD US OFF.

Africa, Asia, Australia, and New Zealand

STRANGEOMETER

CREEPINESS		20/25
SUPERPOWERS		10/25
BUG BEAUTY		17/25
FIGHT FACTOR		25/25
STRANGEOMETER SCORE		72/100

LOCUST

Locusts travel in groups called swarms. There can be up to 80 million locusts in one swarm!

Swarms of locusts eat all of the crops they pass over, causing devastation. They will gobble up everything in sight – fruit, flowers, even clothes hanging on a clothesline.

When food has run out, that doesn't stop them – they then turn to eating each other!

#15

The asp caterpillar is also known as a puss caterpillar because it looks like a cuddly little cat. Other people say it looks like a wig! It later turns into a southern flannel moth.

North and Central America

STRANGEOMETER

 CREEPINESS — 8/25

 SUPERPOWERS — 18/25

 BUG BEAUTY — 22/25

 FIGHT FACTOR — 25/25

 STRANGEOMETER SCORE — 73/100

If an asp drops on you, remove its stingers with tape, then wash with soap and water and put an ice pack on the stings.

ASP CATERPILLAR

These fluffy little creatures may look cute, but you should never touch one – their hairs will give you a very painful sting!

I'M SOMETIMES CALLED A WOOLY SLUG!

You don't want to get behind an asp caterpillar. The trigger-happy critters fire poop pellets out of their bodies at a speed of 4.3 ft. (1.3 m) per second. Yuck!

#14

SCORPION

Scorpions have been around for hundreds of millions of years. There are almost 2,000 species, and 30 to 40 species are poisonous enough to kill a person.

Scorpions glow green under ultraviolet light, such as moonlight. Scientists don't know why. It's a mystery!

STRANGEOMETER

CREEPINESS		20/25
SUPERPOWERS		19/25
BUG BEAUTY		10/25
FIGHT FACTOR		25/25
STRANGEOMETER SCORE		74/100

IF WE HAVE TO, WE CAN SURVIVE BY EATING JUST ONE INSECT A YEAR!

All continents except Antarctica

The sting of the deathstalker scorpion contains about 100 different types of poison.

PUSS MOTH CATERPILLAR

#13

When puss moth caterpillars are disturbed, they rear their heads upwards. Their markings – a red ring and two black dots – look like a big face with a wide-open mouth. It isn't really a face, but it's enough to give any attacker a scare!

STRANGEOMETER

CREEPINESS		19/25
SUPERPOWERS		13/25
BUG BEAUTY		23/25
FIGHT FACTOR		20/25
STRANGEOMETER SCORE		75/100

Puss moth caterpillars turn into a moth that is soft and furry like a cat.

WE SQUIRT ACID AT OUR ENEMIES.

Look for puss moth caterpillars on willow, aspen, and poplar trees. They make hard cocoons out of bits of bark.

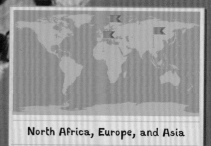

North Africa, Europe, and Asia

53

#12

Female thorn bugs lay around 100 eggs at a time. Baby thorn bugs are the size of sesame seeds.

Thorn bugs are masters of disguise. Their bright colors show up-close, but farther away, they actually make them really hard to see.

WE SUCK THE SAP FROM PLANTS TO SURVIVE.

All continents except Antarctica

THORN BUG

Looking like a spiky thorn helps these bugs avoid getting eaten by birds and large insects.

Thorn bugs talk to each other by making the plant they are standing on vibrate. Humans can't hear their calls unless a special microphone is attached to the plant. Some people say their calls sound like whale songs.

STRANGEOMETER

 CREEPINESS — 22/25

 SUPERPOWERS — 20/25

 BUG BEAUTY — 25/25

 FIGHT FACTOR — 9/25

 STRANGEOMETER SCORE — 76/100

#11

FIREFLY

Fireflies talk to each other using light signals, with a language made up of steady glows and flashes. Different kinds of firefly make different patterns of light – some species all blink on and off at the same time.

All continents except Antarctica

STRANGEOMETER

 CREEPINESS — 23/25

 SUPERPOWERS — 25/25

 BUG BEAUTY — 25/25

 FIGHT FACTOR — 4/25

 STRANGEOMETER SCORE — 77/100

Firefly larvae like to eat snails and worms. Adult fireflies prefer nectar or pollen, although some don't eat anything at all!

Some firefly larvae glow, even those that live underground or underwater. It's to let predators know they don't taste very nice.

There are around 2,000 species of firefly.

If you touch a light bulb, you might get burned, but fireflies can mix oxygen with a substance called luciferin inside their bodies. This creates something called cold light. If a firefly heated up like a light bulb, it wouldn't live very long!

QUIZ

What creepy-crawly is this?

4.

1.
What is the world's biggest spider?

2.
How do thorn bugs talk to each other?

3.
What does a puss moth caterpillar's markings look like?

6. What will locusts eat if they can't find their usual food?

What is the largest wasp in the world?

7.

8.

5.

What can asp caterpillars fire?

What creepy-crawlies are these?

10.

9.

Where can you find the giant weta?

What insect talks using flashing lights?

#10

If you find this huge insect a bit scary, don't worry – it only lives for a week.

OUR LARVAE CAN BREATHE IN AND OUT OF THE WATER!

Eastern dobsonflies have a wingspan of around 5 in. (12.5 cm), making them as big as a chocolate bar. The males also have 1.5 in. long (4 cm long) jaws, but they can't use them to bite – they are too long.

EASTERN DOBSONFLY

Eastern dobsonflies lay up to 3,000 eggs at a time, usually close to a fast-flowing stream. The female covers the eggs with a white fluid, which makes the pile look a bit like bird poop!

North America, Central America, and South America

After hatching, the eastern dobsonfly's young look like this. They are now called larvae and need to live in water. They attach themselves to an air bubble, which helps them float or swim to a safe space, often under some rocks.

STRANGEOMETER

 CREEPINESS — 25/25

 SUPERPOWERS — 10/25

 BUG BEAUTY — 25/25

 FIGHT FACTOR — 18/25

 STRANGEOMETER SCORE — 78/100

The eggs of the eastern dobsonfly always hatch at night.

#9

IF YOU DISTURB ME, I SQUEAK LIKE A MOUSE!

In the past, people were afraid of the death's-head hawkmoth because of its scary markings. It is said that Great Britain's King George III became ill when he discovered two of them in his bedroom!

STRANGEOMETER

 CREEPINESS — 25/25

 SUPERPOWERS — 19/25

 BUG BEAUTY — 25/25

 FIGHT FACTOR — 10/25

STRANGEOMETER SCORE — 79/100

Europe, Africa, and Asia

The death's-head hawkmoth raids beehives to steal yummy honey. They are not afraid of all the busy, stinging bees! Strangely, the bees usually ignore them – scientists think the moths might make themselves smell like bees as a disguise.

DEATH'S-HEAD HAWKMOTH

The death's-head hawkmoth gets its name from the skull-like markings on its body.

LEAF INSECT

These amazing insects disguise themselves as leaves to hide from predators. Some of the "leaves" even have pretend bite marks around the edges!

WE SCATTER OUR EGGS ON THE GROUND — THEY HATCH IN THE SPRING.

Some leaf insects sway from side to side, like a leaf blowing in the wind. They are such masters of disguise that the insects have been known to accidentally take a bite out of one of their friends!

Female leaf insects usually have large wings but can't actually fly. Though the males have smaller wings, they can take to the skies.

Indian Ocean, parts of mainland South Asia and Southeast Asia, Papua New Guinea, and Australia

STRANGEOMETER

CREEPINESS		10/25
SUPERPOWERS		25/25
BUG BEAUTY		25/25
FIGHT FACTOR		20/25
STRANGEOMETER SCORE		80/100

GLASSWING BUTTERFLY

With its transparent wings that seem to be made of glass, this beautiful butterfly is like something out of a fairy tale. In fact, scientists are studying these wings in order to design phone screens that won't reflect light.

> MY SEE-THROUGH WINGS ARE LIKE AN INVISIBILITY CLOAK TO HELP ME HIDE FROM PREDATORS.

STRANGEOMETER

CREEPINESS		23/25
SUPERPOWERS		25/25
BUG BEAUTY		25/25
FIGHT FACTOR		8/25
STRANGEOMETER SCORE		81/100

Central and South America

The glasswing butterfly may look fragile but it's strong and fast – it can carry nearly 40 times its own weight and fly up to 13 mph (8 kph).

BIRD-DUNG CRAB SPIDER

Nobody wants to eat poop, which is why this spider disguises itself as bird droppings. It really makes an effort – not only does it look disgusting, but it smells like dung as well!

WE LIVE AT THE EDGES OF FORESTS IN SOUTHEAST ASIA.

Southeast Asia

This spider spends a lot of time in the open catching flies, which is why it needs a disguise to prevent it from getting eaten by birds. Sometimes it even sits on a piece of its own white silk, to mimic dried bird poop.

STRANGEOMETER

CREEPINESS	24/25
SUPERPOWERS	23/25
BUG BEAUTY	25/25
FIGHT FACTOR	10/25
STRANGEOMETER SCORE	82/100

#5

GIANT
SILKWORM MOTH
CATERPILLAR

Known as the world's deadliest caterpillar, this creature has hairs that are poisonous enough to kill a human.

Once the caterpillar has turned into a moth, it is no longer poisonous and only lives for a few days.

We've killed lots of people, especially in Brazil.

South America

Giant silkworm moth caterpillars are usually around 2 in. (5 cm) long but can grow as big as a human hand. They are found on the bark of trees in the rainforests of South America.

STRANGEOMETER

 CREEPINESS — 20/25

 SUPERPOWERS — 20/25

 BUG BEAUTY — 20/25

 FIGHT FACTOR — 23/25

STRANGEOMETER SCORE — 83/100

#4 ASSASSIN BUG

There are around 7,000 species of assassin bug. They all have dagger-like beaks that they use to attack their prey and suck their bodies dry.

Some assassin bugs are called kissing bugs, because they sometimes bite humans around the lips.

One freaky kind of assassin bug likes to stick the bodies of its victims all over its own body. Gruesome! The insect can carry as many as 20 dead ants at a time.

One type of assassin bug is called the masked hunter. It can disguise itself as a harmless ball of dust. Its body and legs are covered with sticky hairs that catch bits of lint and fluff. It hangs out in houses, feasting on bedbugs and flies. It has been known to bite people as well!

USUALLY WE ARE BROWN AND BLACK, BUT SOMETIMES WE'RE BRIGHTLY COLORED.

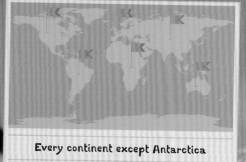

Every continent except Antarctica

STRANGEOMETER

 CREEPINESS — 25/25

 SUPERPOWERS — 20/25

 BUG BEAUTY — 20/25

 FIGHT FACTOR — 19/25

 STRANGEOMETER SCORE — 84/100

BRAZILIAN TREEHOPPER

The freaky Brazilian treehopper looks a bit like an alien helicopter. Nobody knows what those balls on its head are actually for.

Some scientists think the balls on its head might protect the Brazilian treehopper from predators. Perhaps the weird headgear makes it hard to grab.

STRANGEOMETER

CREEPINESS		25/25
SUPERPOWERS		25/25
BUG BEAUTY		25/25
FIGHT FACTOR		10/25
STRANGEOMETER SCORE		85/100

WE LIVE ON A PLANT CALLED A GLORY BUSH.

South America

The forest-dwelling Brazilian treehopper is one of 3,200 species of treehoppers. treehoppers suck sap out of plants with a sharp beak like a straw.

Only the adults are colorful. Young devil's flower mantises are brown and pretend to be boring dried leaves instead of beautiful flowers.

STRANGEOMETER

 CREEPINESS   25/25

 SUPERPOWERS   25/25

 BUG BEAUTY   25/25

 FIGHT FACTOR   18/25

 STRANGEOMETER SCORE   93/100

The ancient Greeks believed mantises had magical powers. They thought that the spit of a mantis could make you blind. They also thought if a horse ate a mantis, the horse would die.

FEMALE MANTISES SOMETIMES BITE OFF THE HEADS OF THEIR MALE PARTNERS!

DEVIL'S FLOWER MANTIS

This beautiful creature pretends to be a flower in order to attract small flying insects, then quickly snatches them out of the air.

Africa

EXPLODING ANT

It may look small and harmless, but this creepy-crawly has an extreme way of protecting its home and its family. If it feels threatened, it explodes, killing itself and covering its enemy with poisonous goo!

Of all the defense tactics you may have heard about, the exploding ant's self-destruct skill is the most extreme! The Malaysian exploding ant is different from most other bugs because it sacrifices itself for the good of its colony. Scientists call this *autothysis*, a word that comes from the Greek words for *self* and *sacrifice*.

Ants always look out for their fellow ants, and by exploding, they can scare off competitors or predators and save their colony.

Malaysia and Brunei

When the ant explodes, it dies, and sometimes the invading insect dies, too. If the ant's attacker (usually another ant) survives, it learns to stay well away from this kind of ant in the future!

Scientists have found that it doesn't take much to make an exploding ant blow itself up – just a light touch will do.

I AIM MY GOO AT MY ENEMY'S FACE!

When it senses danger, the ant contracts its abdomen, causing its poison glands to explode.

STRANGEOMETER

 CREEPINESS   25/25

 SUPERPOWERS   25/25

 BUG BEAUTY   25/25

 FIGHT FACTOR   25/25

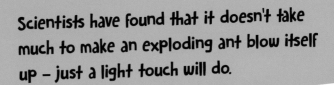 STRANGEOMETER SCORE   100/100

QUIZ

See if you can answer these questions on the ten creepy-crawlies you've just learned about!

1.

What creepy-crawly is this?

3.

Leaf insects are such masters of disguise that they sometimes do what?

How many more times its own body weight can the glasswing butterfly carry?

4.

How did the death's-head hawkmoth get its name?

2.

6. What does the assassin bug stick to its body?

What creepy-crawly is this?

8. What are the balls on a Brazilian treehopper's head for?

7.

5. What is the world's deadliest caterpillar?

10. Why does the exploding ant explode?

9. What powers did the ancient Greeks think the devil's flower mantis had?

ANSWERS

1. EASTERN DOBSONFLY 2. FROM THE SKULL-SHAPED MARKING ON ITS BODY 3. TAKE A BITE OUT OF EACH OTHER! 4. 40 TIMES MORE! 5. THE GIANT SILKWORM MOTH CATERPILLAR 6. BIRD-DUNG CRAB SPIDER 7. THE BODIES OF ITS VICTIMS 8. NOBODY KNOWS, BUT THEY MAY BE TO MAKE THEM HARDER FOR PREDATORS TO GRAB 9. THEY THOUGHT ITS SPIT COULD BLIND YOU AND THAT A HORSE WOULD DIE IF IT ATE ONE 10. TO PROTECT ITS HOME AND FAMILY

GLOSSARY

abdomen	the part of the body between the chest and hips
camouflage	a way of making something look like its surroundings so it can't be seen
cocoon	a covering made to protect baby insects as they grow
cyborg	a human whose body has been taken over by a mechanical or electronic device
decibel	a measurement of sound
fungus	a class of organism (living thing) that is neither plant nor animal
g-force	the measurement of force felt by a body when it accelerates
gland	an organ in the body that produces substances that help the body function
larva	a grub or caterpillar, hatched from an egg; the young form of many insects
mammal	warm-blooded animals that breathe air; the females have glands that produce milk for their young
nectar	a liquid made by plants to attract bees, which they use to make honey
orbit	the path an object takes around a particular point
parasite	an organism (living thing) that lives on and feeds off another organism
pollen	a fine yellow dust produced by a plant that helps it form seeds
predator	an animal that hunts and eats other another animals
rainforest	a warm tropical forest with high rainfall
sap	the juice of a plant
transparent	see-through